Worst Practices in… Corporate Training

By Jim Glantz

Illustrated by Mark Sean Wilson

Contact us at www.taflat.com for permission requests and to get electronic or editable versions of the documents included in the book.
Printed in the United States of America
First Edition

ACKNOWLEDGEMENTS

I'd like to acknowledge the trainers and their teams who contributed their painful stories of training disasters. We had laughs, and shed some tears.

Also I'd like to acknowledge my team, Talia Seehoff and Mark Sean Wilson for their dedication to taking this book over the finish line!

Thanks also to my many mentors and career supporters: Lori Stutsman, Pat Wadors, Toni Cusumano, Kevin Walsh, Craig Cooper, Garrett Cash, and Kia Michel. You all are the best at what you do, and give selflessly to others' success!

And most of all, thanks to my family and friends for their boundless support and love!

Thank you!

TABLE OF CONTENTS

PREFACE (OTHERWISE KNOWN AS THE SECTION NO ONE READS…)

I'm a picky guy – I know this about myself. And that's very good for you, the reader. What it means is that you will learn from my years of critiquing others and myself. When you finish this book, my goal is for you say to yourself, "I learned so much that will help me actually DO my work!"

When I started writing this book almost six years ago, I envisioned a kind-of training manual for professionals. I initially thought the best way to instill confidence in training professionals would be to provide them with a step-by-step instruction book for developing great training programs, complete with templates and checklists. After about two months of writing this book, I remembered a quote from a Situational Leadership course I had taught years ago…

"Direction feels like support when the person is new to the task."

The flip side of that axiom, it seems to me, is that when someone is not new to a task, they need support and wisdom...and wisdom so often comes from mistakes.

"You don't learn to walk by following rules. You learn by doing, and by falling over."
Richard Branson

These ideas further crystallized during a conversation with a good friend, who has been a Real Estate professional for years, when he comically stated, "You know, it's true that it's helpful to learn from your mistakes; but…it's so much better to learn from others' mistakes!"

After that comment, I decided to scrap the work I'd developed on an instructive-guidebook, and to pivot to writing an entire book dedicated to fascinating stories of "Failures," "Disasters," and "Ways in which Training Professionals Have Altogether Messed Up." As I grinned from ear to ear at the thought of this topic, I contacted Corporate Trainers on LinkedIn and in my professional network, with the fun goal of hearing their disastrous stories.

Now, I've always hated business books. Mainly because I find that business books are full of "the right way to do things," and the authors tell great personal success stories. Perhaps they do that because the authors hope to be hired as consultants by their readers, and, the consultants probably believe that no one would hire them if they actually aired their dirty laundry, their disaster stories.

But that's what we've been missing! And that's what is so fun and meaningful, from a learning perspective!

So, I promise, this book will not be boring!

The book's structure will include lessons on the 4 Phases of Training (Needs, Design, Implementation, and Sustainment), and I've provided you with chances to take notes directly within the book.

Worst Practices in... Corporate Training includes a compilation of the best stories of failures from dozens of honest interviews with training professionals. These professionals were nice enough to bear their souls, and I was nice enough not to include their names. Of course, while these stories will result in many cringe worthy moments, the stories illustrate numerous lessons. The most important lesson is that you often learn more from your failures than from your successes!

You might be interested to know that all of the of the trainers interviewed for this book are highly successful in their careers, and each one was shown, and found solace in, the wise graphic below:

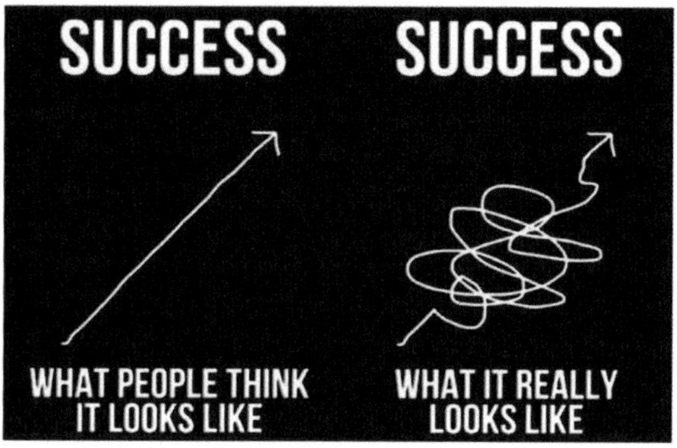

HOW TO USE THIS BOOK

What This Book Is Not About

If what you'd like to learn is what training theories are helpful, please put this book down. I will not be discussing training theories like Knowles' Adult Learning Principles. Nor will I emphasize Kirkpatrick's evaluation model. Nor will I teach you the ADDIE Model – an acronym that most of us have taken to writing on cheat sheet post-it notes in our pockets so that we can remember what each of the words stand for. In this book, you will only learn practical training lessons.

What This Book Is About

What this book does is to provide an overview framework for putting together a great training program, and recommendations for each part of the structure. In addition, this book provides stories of what could happen when one does not follow these steps.

Each story of failure will be placed in the section where the root cause of that failure occurred. So, for example, if one of our interviewee's training sessions failed because s/he didn't gain sufficient senior-level commitment to the training at the onset, that story will be placed in the first phase of training programs, "Understanding the Business Case and Objectives (with the training sponsor)."

In addition, for each section of the book, I have included a checklist of lessons learned and critical questions to ask/get answered before transitioning to the next phase of a training program.

Please use this book as your handbook and keep a pen with you. There will be numerous opportunities for you to jot down your own notes, thoughts, and learnings.

Great training relies on both the art of the training's architect and on the facile skills of the trainer. But it also relies on the clear support of the organization. This book can be a way for you to identify potential pitfalls, understand why these pitfalls take place, and give you the chance to plan for them…proactively. That way, you will have fewer stories of failures and more stories of marvelous successes!

TERMS AND DEFINITIONS

Course Design – A section-by-section course layout, including objectives for each section, key topics and timing for each section, and even speaker's notes written out in bullet points for each section.

Skill Sustainment Strategy – A structured, post-training plan to support the skills learned during the training. Skill Sustainment Strategies include ways to encourage (or mandate) new behaviors back on the job. Oftentimes, these strategies are woven into new job evaluation criteria or Performance Management systems.

Soft Skills - Soft skills are a combination of interpersonal people skills, social skills, communication skills, character traits, attitudes, and emotional intelligence. Soft skills tend to help people effectively navigate their environment, work well with others, perform well, and achieve their goals with complementing hard skills (technical or functional skills).

Training Communication Plan – A structured project plan for communicating training, that relies of "cascading sponsorship" – that is, the first message comes from the most senior sponsor of the training, showing his/her support for the training. Subsequent messages "cascade" down from less senior sponsors such as department heads who encourage their staffs to attend the training.

Training Logistics Plan – A structured project plan to manage all training logistics, including training materials printing & kitting, room reservations, A/V equipment, food and drinks, and numerous other details that must be managed to pull off successful training.

Training Strategy – The overall training strategy, including objectives and details about each audience.

Section One: Understanding the Need (for the Training)

ESTABLISHING THE BUSINESS DRIVER & THE ART OF LISTENING AND FACILITATING CONVERSATIONS

"You cannot truly listen to anyone and do anything else at the same time."
– **M. Scott Peck**

Perhaps the greatest challenge for a trainer, and the greatest opportunity, is working with their organizational leaders to understand the business need for the training. Whether training technical skills or so-called "soft skills," leaders often just say to trainers, "Would you give us a training on X?"

From my experience and personal reflection, most of us who enter into the field of Training are doers. We hear the business leaders' request and want to launch right into developing and delivering the course. And, even better, if we have the course already prepared, we're ready to tell the business leader a date when we can deliver!

So, while the business leader is saying that he or she would like to improve their department's communications, our "guns are loaded" like Yosemite Sam, and we're ready to start firing!

What's the problem with that?

The problem is, we are respected professionals, and we know better.

We know we should ask probing questions…and we know we should spend some time listening. It's in every trainer's handbook, right?

"Define your training objectives" and "Understand the Business Driver" — we've heard these clichés so often, we often dismiss this step and believe that we know better.

STRATEGIC PHASES OF TRAINING

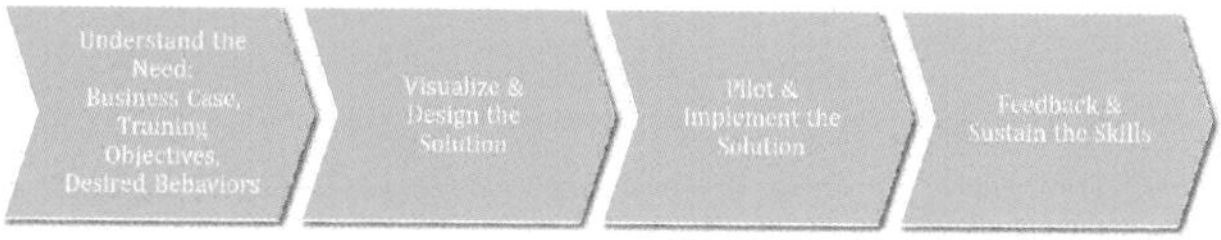

"Sure," you ask, "Is now the time when you tell me that you always get the business need before launching training?"

Nope, let's hear a story about the opposite…

Our first "story of failure" comes to us from a Vice President of Training at a multi-billion dollar company. This V.P. (whom we'll call Jennifer) was gracious enough to tell us this story about when she did NOT do it right. She added her own title for this story, "Jumping Right In – The Eager Beaver!"

Enjoy this first cringeworthy story, from Jennifer…

Jumping Right In – The Eager Beaver

As a new V.P. of Training, I wanted nothing more than to prove my worth by providing high quality training, and faster than expected. So, when a senior executive graced me by popping by my office and requesting training, I jumped right in!

As I sipped my late-morning coffee, pondering the training programs I wanted to launch at this new company, the Company's CIO stopped by to pay me an unscheduled visit.

This senior executive delivered a broad, welcoming smile, and proceeded to tell me that he had heard great things about the DISC (or Communication Styles) workshop that my team had recently provided to other departments in the Company. He then asked if my team could deliver a DISC workshop for his staff.

Was I excited! Not only did my team and I just receive a great compliment, this request was proof of my team's worth – the organization was "pulling" for our training, versus us "pushing" training out to them. Perfect for my teams' job security!

Rather than ask, "What is your objective?" or "What areas of improvement are you specifically looking for?" I almost yelled in excited, "Sure, when would you like to do it?" I did not pause to ask questions to clarify objectives, but rather I had just committed to a date for **delivering** on these unknown objectives!

By the end of that week, the CIO's entire team had taken the online DISC assessment (at $40 per assessment), and we were ready to launch the workshop.

The following week, we delivered our one-day DISC workshop for the CIO's entire senior team. The CIO couldn't attend the training, due to an "important meeting." But no matter…I didn't even question that telltale sign.

The instructor and I thought the workshop went fine, as these workshops usually did. Feedback at the end of the day was positive, and everyone said they learned a lot…and enjoyed themselves. Though, admittedly, we did not identify any major breakthroughs.

After the training, I couldn't wait to get the CIO's feedback…and more compliments! I was anticipating a doubling-down on the same positive feedback he had provided earlier about my team and me. Unfortunately, that was not what I received.

The CIO told me, quite blandly, that he had heard people say fairly good things about the workshop.

"However," he added, "I have not noticed any improvements to their email communications, nor in their communication styles with customers."

“Oh,” I replied, “I didn’t know you were looking for those two objectives. You mentioned you wanted a DISC workshop.”

“Yes,” he replied, “I wanted a DISC workshop to help my team improve their email writing and customer communication. I think I mentioned that.”

In my haste to jump in, I had not asked the CIO his objectives for the training. Even worse, if he was right, I had not even heard the CIO mention those objectives during that same conversation. Truthfully, I’m confident that the CIO never mentioned his objectives in our meeting. However, without any notes or an email follow-up on my part, I had no leg to stand on.

It’s the training expert’s job to develop and deliver excellent training…it is not the CIO’s job. I wasn’t about to use the excuse, “I remember that conversation differently,” because that comment only serves to show a lack of self-awareness.

UGH!!! So painful!

Your Notes: What did you learn from this story? How will this failure help you to develop your future training projects?

Our second "story of failure" comes from a lengthy interview with Robert, who was in charge of all Training and Communications for a major software roll-out at a $10b electronics manufacturer, with over 20,000 employees located in over 9 countries. Robert now is a highly successful Chief Learning Officer. However, he admits, his path to glory wasn't always filled with successes.

In the story below, Robert describes a massive failure in Training and Communication that he attributes to the first phase of training: "Understanding the Need: Business Case, Training Objectives, and Desired Behaviors."

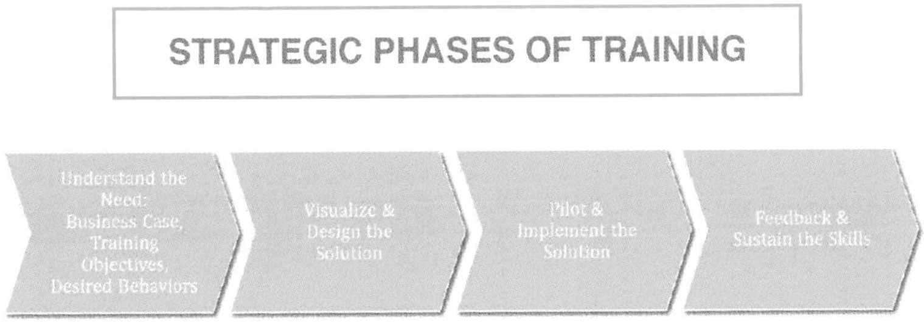

In this story, Robert claims that he made two crucial, and fatal, mistakes:

1) Robert did not clearly create and communicate a compelling business case, so that others behaved the way the Company needed them to behave.

2) Robert did not understand that the behaviors that were needed for people to use the new software system directly contradicted the Company norms… and even contradicted the Company's incentive policies!

Story 2

Uh-Oh! We've Got G.A.S. – "Go Around the System"

I had just been promoted to Sr. Manager of Training at a large high-tech electronics manufacturing company in the Silicon Valley, in California. At that time, the Dot.Com businesses were booming, and it was understood that once you made Director at our Company, you would be a millionaire within four years. I was so close I could taste it! But, it was not to be…

With more money comes more responsibility, and I'd just been given the lead role on the Change Management (Training and Communications) track of our major software implementation. This type of software, known as an ERP system or Enterprise Resource Planning, effected every Manufacturing, Operations, Engineering, and Finance position in the Company.

Believe it or not, in the year 2000, ERP systems were a fairly new phenomenon, and the Training/ Change Management community hadn't learned all of our lessons about rolling out these systems. Those of us implementing the systems back then made ***a lot*** of mistakes -- so those of us still doing the job today don't have to.

After almost ten years of Training experience, I had become a solid Trainer. I also had the logistics portion of Training down-cold. I created my project plans in MS Project, and I input every task, dependency, resource, and expected date. I know it may sound like bragging, but I was excellent at organizing the details. And, for a project with so many people impacted across the entire world, I knew the "devil was in the details"!

What I didn't know was that the devil also lurked in the big picture. In this case, I assumed that everyone knew how important this software implementation was, and I had good reason to believe that. This software project was a direct order from the Board of Directors and our CEO, who also happened to be the co-Founder of the company. I mean, you don't get better senior sponsor support than that! The Board knew that for our Company to grow, we needed a large, robust software system – a system that allowed for cross-sharing of knowledge through our 18 business units. We needed this system to roll-up our financial information, plan the annual production of all of our products, and to intelligently report the health of our business to Wall Street. As a public company, that last point was crucial.

So, by the time I got the nod to take on this critical Change Management/Training track, I assumed that everyone had received these business points. I assumed they would be ready to accept the rollout and attend all training to get themselves and their teams ready. I saw my job as a Training Manager – to create all training materials and build a superb project plan that made sure every last detail was ready. So, my small team and I worked in our "War Room," in Headquarters, and created our materials and project plans.

We did an excellent job at what we thought was our job. However, we never once got out of our office and asked the Engineers and Manufacturing employees how much they had heard about this software project. Although we drafted beautiful PowerPoint slides that described the business case and rollout plan for the project, we never once presented that business case directly to the line employees, or even to the junior executives.

What's more, we never asked the employees whether they understood or agreed with the business case for this project. Had we even talked with the Vice Presidents in the 18 businesses, we would have found that the Board and CEO had spent no time with them, apart from an email that went out to announce the project.

So, without completing Phase One of the Strategic Phases of Training, we leapt right into Phase Two: "Visualize and Define the Solution." We did our visualization. We planned detailed scenarios for training, with step-by-step job aids and instructions for how to navigate this software system. We prepared gorgeous training manuals and feedback forms. We followed our logistics plans to a tee, and, just before the system was to go live, we sent out training emails and launched our training.

And that's the moment we realized we were about to fail in a most spectacular fashion.

Our first training session was with our Volume

Manufacturing division in Texas. We flew from California Headquarters several days early to set up the logistics (classrooms, Audio-Visuals, training laptops, food, and more). Our training emails had been delivered, and we were ready.

The first class we taught was attended by about 1/3 of the invited audience. When we asked those who were there what they thought, they shrugged and told us they were extremely busy at this time of year, cranking out machines. I wondered if they even knew that, without this training, in three months they would not be able to manufacture machines if they didn't know how to use the ERP system. In any event, we delivered the training to those who were there.

For the second class, we had even fewer attendees. Only 5 of the 20 invited employees made it. That pattern repeated for the third class, and I called my Director in California to let her know what was going on and that I was beginning to get nervous. My Director said she would call the VP of Operations there, and see what was going on.

Two days later, my Director asked me what communications had been sent to the employees, including to the VP of Operations. I walked her through our detailed Communication Plan, and she seemed satisfied that I was organized in my planning. Then my Director told me some bad news. The VP of Operations said he knew ***about*** the system, but didn't seem clear with ***why*** we needed it. In his mind, everything was working fine — we were making record numbers of machines, sales were through the roof, and our stock was soaring.

After much discussion with my Director, the VP of Operations agreed to send out an email telling everyone to show up to training.

Now at least we knew why people at Manufacturing hadn't been showing up to training. However, our problems didn't stop there.

For the fourth class, my team and I prepared to deliver the Engineering module to the high-tech Engineers. Just about everyone showed up for the training, and now I wished that they hadn't!

The Engineering module involved training the Engineers of the Electronics and Physics Research and Development Departments. To use this part of the software system, the Engineers needed to upload into the system their "Works-in-Progress" or "WIPs" -- schematics/designs. This requirement meant that others who would manufacture the high-tech equipment would have early access to these schematics during the Research and Development phase. The idea was that with more time and access to the Engineers' plans, Manufacturing Engineers could understand the plans and could create their own schematics to be ready to build that equipment.

(I know, …we're getting in the weeds here, so let me just get to it, and I'll explain what happened.)

What I did not anticipate was this…Engineers earn their money in several ways:

1) They earn a salary like regular employees.

2) They receive stock grants from the Company, tied to the Company's success.

3) They are allowed to retain their Intellectual Property licenses on all of their engineering designs developed for research. For the best Engineers, this 3rd form of compensation was the most lucrative. I hadn't known anything about that!

What all that meant was these brilliant, highly specialized Engineers often were competing with each other, and rushing to patent their new research ideas before others in their field. And here I was standing in front of them, showing them a dandy software system that required them to share these same ideas with other engineers, while the ideas were still works-in-progress… or, more to the point, before they had been patented!

Uh, well, that didn't go well.

During the training, Kumar, one of the engineers said to me:

"So, let me get this straight, Robert. You're asking me to post my WIPs into the shared folder, so that it is viewable by everyone, while still in progress?"

"Yes," I beamed.

"I see," Kumar replied.

Kumar did not speak another word during the training. He sat very politely, listened, and even followed the computer clicks, as required, on the training site. None of the other engineers, similarly, said a word.

It wasn't until almost two months later, when I discovered what stinky pile of dog-doo I had stepped in. And I found out accidentally.

I was having lunch with two of the Engineers who had been friendly and helpful during the entire software project. They smiled, and quietly said, "You know why no one is uploading their WIPs into this system, right?" "No," I gasped. "Well, let us tell you…"

And that was how I learned that my software system had been doomed from the very start.

Your Notes: What did you learn from this story? How will this failure help you to develop your future training projects?

Below are some key questions to ask during Phase 1 of a training program:

Areas to Cover	**Questions to Ask**
Your Opening Questions: Business Driver Burning Platform	Why do you want to hold this training? What business need(s) are you trying to solve through this training effort? Are there any reasons that can inform the timing for when this training should be delivered?
More Questions to Ask: Behavior Questions	What specifically do you want your employees to do, do differently, or do better, as a result of this training? Will there be any reasons that people will resist these new behaviors?
Define the Business Case: Behavior Questions	How will the actual business improve if your staff is behaving the way you've described before?
If time permits, conduct this activity: Jointly create a list of desired behaviors {You may want to create your list first and set up a separate meeting to compare your list with that of your business leader.}	Let's create a specific list of actual behaviors you'd like to see.

Tips	
Active Listening	○Listen carefully to the business leader, with minimal interruptions other than for clarification. ○Remember that while identifying training behavioral results comes naturally to us, many times the business leader has never had the chance to think through the specific behaviors they would like to see. ○Believe in them, and trust that they will get there. Be encouraging and patient.
Take Notes…these examples are GOLD for your training	○Note that you'll be able to use these business examples during the training. ○These examples will be helpful to illustrate the specific behaviors that the training hopes to generate.
Use Notes for the Executive Kick-Off	○Modify your notes into PowerPoint slides that you can use for the executive to kick-off the training ○Ask the executive/business leader if s/he would be willing to discuss the business case as a kick off to the training!

Handy Tool – To Help with Understanding the Need for Training

Use the checklist below* to keep track of what questions you need to ask and what information you need to get before starting the next phase of training.

Question	Kind of Information Wanted
Why do you want to hold this training?	Business Driver behind wanting the training
What business need(s) are you trying to solve through this training effort?	Burning Platform to build off of
What specifically do you want your employees to do, do differently, or do better, as a result of this training?	Vision and core objectives of the training
Let's create a specific list of actual behaviors you'd like to see.	Desired new behaviors and outcomes of the training
Are there any reasons that can inform the timing for when this training should be delivered?	Practical information regarding implementation

* Contact us at www.taflat.com to get electronic or editable versions of these tables.

Section Two: Visualize and Design the Solution

YOUR VISION WILL SHAPE THE FUTURE

"I had a clear vision of myself winning the Mr. Universe contest. It was a very spiritual thing, in a way, because I had such faith in the route, the path, that there was never a question in my mind that I would make it."

- Arnold Schwarzenegger

STRATEGIC PHASES OF TRAINING

We all like to "get stuff done" — it makes us feel accomplished. While those levels of motivation will likely propel you to a certain amount of success in your career, it may be just that quality that holds you back from that executive role you've always wanted. The art of visualization requires counter-intuitive advice: do less and think more.

In the world of Training, once we've understood our training requirements, we then need to allow ourselves time to think…and…to ***do nothing***. We need to let the stew simmer. Might I recommend taking a stroll? Or meditating? Or, really, whatever settles you down. Allow your imagination to paint a picture of what your training could be like, and will be like, for the participants. Try to picture yourself sitting in the class and imagine what you would like to experience — probably a bit of lecture, a chance to get up and use flip charts, capture your own thoughts, and share practical ideas with others in the session.

Anyway, you'll know you have developed a fabulous vision when you are imagining a course that YOU would want to take. You know that you'll need to budget plenty of time for participants to practice their newly-learned skills and to discuss with others how they will use what they have learned.

Our next "story of failure" comes from a trainer who was hired by one of the premier leadership-training firms in the world, located in beautiful Santa Barbara, California. This trainer (who we'll call Richard) was asked, as his first assignment, to shadow one of the Master Trainers at one of their 2-day leadership programs offered to the public. During the interview for this book, Richard was painfully honest about his experience.

The program that Richard was asked to learn so that he could teach it himself someday, clearly had been developed by people who lacked vibrant imaginations. Richard's reactions are priceless.

Story 3

Consistency is the last refuge of the unimaginative. Oscar Wilde

"They had paid a lot of money to be here." That was the thought that kept going through my mind as the Master Trainer lectured endlessly on the PowerPoint slides that had been provided.

I had just started with a top leadership training firm in Santa Barbara, and I was eager to be paired up with the most respected senior trainer in the Firm. The Firm's goal was to have me learn their training techniques by shadowing this trainer. That way, I would soon be prepared to deliver their training program on my own. For two days, I watched in horror...

The leadership course began with an interactive icebreaker. Participants were asked to jot down their favorite hobby on their "name tents," and then they were asked to turn to the person next to them to share those hobbies. It's a typical icebreaker, but it worked like a charm. Everyone was talking, and you could feel the excitement in the room!

That was the last time in this two-day course that these pairs would be asked to talk with each other.

With excitement bubbling, the senior instructor settled into his lecture much like a paper towel settles over a bowl of water. He began discussing their leadership model, and explained that their model would be the topic for the next two days. Everyone was interested and probably thought that they would soon be asked to respond to this model by discussing their own reactions, and would be asked to consider how to use the framework back with their own businesses.

The instructor was a brilliant person and actually not uninteresting. So, for the first two hours, the students' eyes remained wide. They learned new concepts and heard real stories of companies that had successfully used these leadership principles to turn their businesses around. Really, it was quite interesting.

I can't tell you the exact point at which things changed, but at some point, the students (and I) began to realize that they would never get to talk again for the next two days. The leadership program would continue with the instructor talking for the full duration. I even think the instructor became bored of his own voice, as the once-vibrant tones seemed to lose their richness, subtly fading into a hollow monologue. (You've all been there. You know.)

I looked around the classroom and noticed that the students' eyes reminded me of those lizards with dual eyelids – their eyes were open but it seemed an inner eyelid had closed and shut out the inner monologues in their minds. These professionals sat straight upright and always looked at the instructor, but you could sense that their minds now were occupied with distant thoughts, probably of their next vacation or all the work waiting for them back at the office.

Perhaps the students realized that the next two days would be another boring, unimaginative, almost torturous course.

Even for me, I found my mind drifting to my last vacation in Maui, thinking of scuba diving and large sea turtles, while the instructor went on. I caught myself, and remembered that I was being paid to apprentice and that my role was to listen and learn.

I wondered, "Does he (the instructor) know that he is losing these students? Will he start to read their lackluster energy, and maybe ask them to break into small discussion groups? Will he pull the group together?" After a while, I realized that this brilliant, but unimaginative, instructor would not gain that self-awareness.

I also realized that I would soon need to quit this training firm and find a position that allowed me to deliver training the way I wanted to.

Your Notes: What did you learn from this story? How will this failure help you to develop your future training projects?

Below are some key questions to ask during Phase 2 of a training program:

Areas to Cover	Questions to Ask
Less Training Topics – More Time: ◎ Training Objectives ◎ Training Atmosphere ◎ Time Allowed	◎ Besides learning the skills, do you want the training to provide the participants with time to bond with each other? ◎ Do you envision an interactive course, allowing the students time to practice their skills during the training? ◎ Are you OK with the course taking a little more time to deliver in order to build and practice new skills during the session?
Instructor & Instructional Designer: ◎ Competencies of great instructors ◎ Competencies of great instructional designers	◎ Besides intelligence, is your instructor empathetic and imaginative? ◎ Have you provided your instructional designer (or yourself) with the time and space to do effective visualization?

Tips	
Visualization	Give yourself permission to do NOTHING but DREAM! Provide yourself with time to imagine the students and their jobs.
Less Training Topics	Distill what you want to teach into the shortest list possible. Increase the time to learn each concept on that short list. What skills require practice during the class, and what are the time requirements? For example, your business partner may say that s/he wants to deliver a one-day management course for new managers, and their list of what the managers should learn runs down your entire arm. Work with your business partner to skinny-down that list, hopefully to the top 3-4 things they need to learn.

More Time Allotted for Each Topic – Find Your Training Battle Rhythm	Take your prioritized list, and be sure to give it the proper amount of time. FIND YOUR BATTLE RHYTHM…That is, consider how much time each topic requires for lecture, reflection, practice in small groups, and to debrief as a large group. For new skills, remember to provide time for repetition. For example, if you want the students to learn how to respond with tact to prickly customers, you may need to prepare 4-5 realistic scenarios, and each participant may need to practice 2-3 times in order to form the neurological pathways to respond to each customer scenario.
Get Out and See Their Jobs - "GEMBA"	In LEAN manufacturing, there is a principle called "Gemba," which is a Japanese word for "get out and walk around." In this case, get out to their job sites and visit the people who you will teach. Spend some time asking them questions. Some questions might include: "What would you like to learn to do your job even better that you do now?" "What's the hardest part of your job?" If you cannot get out to their jobs, conduct a few interviews or focus groups to gain their input on the training materials and to capture a few scenarios/ examples that relate to the material.

Take Notes — these examples are GOLD for your training	○ As mentioned in Phase 1, the notes that you capture when you visit your students at their job sites will provide valuable business examples during the training. ○ Create meaningful, real scenarios to illustrate your points and for the students to practice their skills. ○ The notes from your on-the-job research will be critical as a reference.
Self-Reflection	○ After practicing new skills, adult students need some time to reflect on what they learned and how they will apply the skills back on the job. ○ One handy activity is to ask each person to write down specifically how they will use the skills, in the form of a SMART goal. Then, individuals could share their goals in small group discussions.

Handy Tool – To Help with Visualizing/ Designing the Training

1. Key Learning Objectives

• *Describe what Learners should be able to do after the training event.*

2. Audience

• Who is the primary audience for this training?

• Is there a secondary audience, such as the Managers who oversee these individuals?

• Which functions does the audience include?

  ◦ For example, Manufacturing, Quality, Packaging, Warehouse, Distribution and Technical Operations (Technicians, Packaging Engineer).

• Does it make sense to have cross functional groups that work together in the same class?

  ◦ For example, the Manufacturing Supervisor and Quality Supervisor who normally work together)

• What are the demographics of the audience? (E.g. locations, shifts, levels?).

If necessary, provide a summary of the audience statistics. See sample below:*

	TOTAL	Mftg	Quality	Pkg	Whse	Distr	Tech Ops Pkg Eng Ops Cntl
Site #1							
Supervisors/ Technicians							
Managers							
Site #2							
Supervisors/ Pkg Eng							
Managers							
Site #3							
Supervisors/ Tech/Pkg Eng							
Managers							
Site #4							
Supervisors/ Ops Cntl							
Managers							
TOTAL							
Supervisors/ Tech/Pkg Eng/ Ops Cntl							
Managers							

* Contact us at www.taflat.com to get electronic or editable versions of these tables.

3. Timing

• How long should the classes run?

• Is there a sequence in which the audience will be trained?

° For example, is it necessary to train the Managers prior to the Supervisors?

• Will classes be run across multiple shifts to accommodate work schedules?

4. Preliminary Curriculum

<Your Project Name> Curriculum

• If your project requires multiple training events, below is a preliminary curriculum to draft objectives for each course. Each row represents a given course — your detailed course design will be developed by completing the Course Design Template (also located on Open Forum).

• In the table below, list the course name, the objectives for each course, audience, total participants, class capacity, instructor (either a name or a type of instructor), and time to deliver each course.*

Course Name	Learning Objectives	Audience	Total Part.	Max # Part./ Class	Instructor	Timing

* Contact us at www.taflat.com to get electronic or editable versions of these tables.

5. Instructors

• If you do not know the names of the instructors at this point, use this section to describe the type of instructor you require.

° For example: level, internal or external, knowledge level of process, technology, etc.

6. Learning Strategies

• *Consider the Learning Strategies for each course. Does the course require the completion of something prior to the students' arrival, such as a survey or reading materials?*
  ° *Should the course be taught in particular manner, for example employing quizzes, scenarios, or skills practice?*
  ° *After the course, will you require a skill sustainment activity, such as a certification or the completion of a template?*
  ° *In the table below*, list the requirements for each phase of the class.*

	Pre Class	During Class	Post Class
Course Name	• *Is there required pre-work, such as reading or completing a template prior to the class?*	• *Does the class involve lecture, interactive discussion, scenarios, group problem solving, quizzes, etc.?*	• *What follow up activities are required to ensure the learning objectives were achieved?* • *Is Certification required?*

* Contact us at www.taflat.com to get electronic or editable versions of these tables.

7. Training Delivery Approach

• *How will training be delivered?*

• *For example, classroom and instructor-led, shoulder to shoulder (on the job), one-on-one in meeting rooms?*

• *Where will training be delivered? Where will it be located?*

8. Training Development Approach

Design: *How will courses be designed? Who will create the course designs? What will be included in the course design document? Does the course design also include a description of any materials that will be used to support the course activities? Who will review and approve the course designs?*

Development: *Who will develop the course materials? Who will review and approve these materials? What will be included in the course materials? i.e. presentations, templates, flow charts, job aids, etc.?*

Pilot: *Will the course be piloted? The pilot is a way to run through the content and get feedback on the content before it is fully rolled out to all participants. The pilot also provides instructors with a practice run prior to the rollout.*

9. Technology Requirements

- In the table below*, list the technology requirements for each course.

Course	Tech Requirements
Course 1	• *What technology requirements exist for each course?* • *e.g. projectors, laptops, video cameras, DVD players*

* Contact us at www.taflat.com to get electronic or editable versions of these tables.

10. Logistics Requirements

- *What are the logistics requirements for the courses?*
    - *For example, training rooms in various locations that accommodate up to x people, setting up the room in a specific style, adjusting course timing for shift workers*
- *Who will determine training schedules and manage invites?*
- *Refreshments — Water & Snacks?*
- *Who will manage all logistics and materials reproduction?*

11. Maintenance

- *In the table below*, list the maintenance plan for each course.*

Course	Maintenance Plan
Course	• How will new hires be trained on the knowledge taught in the course? • If the process taught in the course changes, who will oversee updates to training materials and who will update all stakeholders on the process changes? • How many times a year will the course be taught? • Are the maintenance activities above included in the right person's goals/job roles and responsibilities?

* Contact us at www.taflat.com to get electronic or editable versions of these tables.

Section Three: Pilot & Implement the Solution (Flawless Execution)

GREAT EXECUTION BEATS GREAT STRATEGY

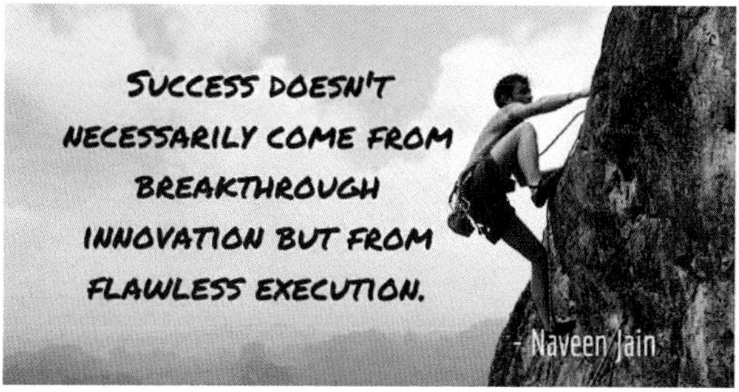

SUCCESS DOESN'T NECESSARILY COME FROM BREAKTHROUGH INNOVATION BUT FROM FLAWLESS EXECUTION.
- Naveen Jain

In a conversation with Stewart Resnick, the self-made billionaire who owns "The Wonderful Company," I asked him what is the one lesson he would tell anyone who works for him. Stewart replied, "I will take *good* strategy and *excellent* execution any day, above *great* strategy and *average* execution." I followed up by asking Stewart, as a practical question, how he knows if he should invest in one of his employee's new strategies, whether it is a Marketing strategy, a new product strategy, or a new Training program. Stewart replied, "I need to see someone successfully pilot their idea on a small scale. Once they can show that success, I'll give them the money to implement on a large scale."

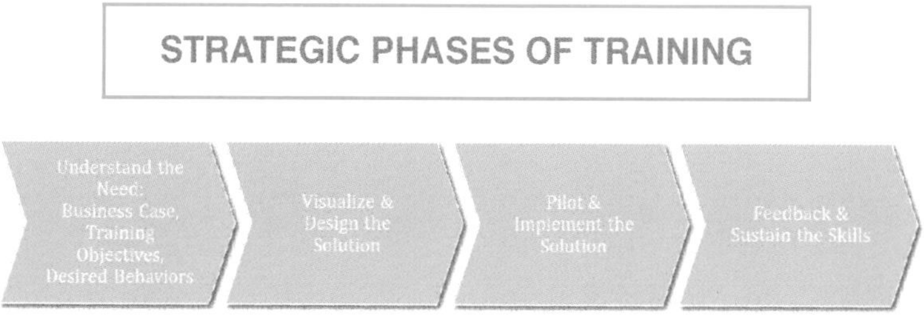

Story 4

"What? No Pilot Session Needed! We got this!"

I had always been a Software Engineer. In India, I received Masters degrees in both Computer Science and Engineering. Now I was the Director of IT Systems for a $5b manufacturing company, specializing in the bottling of salad dressing and other food products. I was excellent at my job.

So, when the VP of Operations asked me to lead the Change Management (Training & Communications) track for a major ERP implementation, I was ready and willing! I was confident that I would be successful in this role, just as I had been successful at IT systems for my entire career.

Whoops.

Our Director of Learning had mentioned to me that ERP system training is as much about explaining process changes as it is about teaching how to use the new technical system. She also explained that I should not underestimate the value of piloting the training to get to know my audience, and that I must assess their understanding of the training well – that way, I would know if I needed to retrain after the software was rolled out.

Hrmphf! I had rolled out training before. You

merely schedule a class, get a projector and some job aids, and begin walking the students through the software clicks! I mean, it was time consuming to get to all students, on all shifts, but I had a sizable team of Software Engineers and we could just divide up the training.

Was I wrong! Here's what happened…

With two weeks before the system was to go live to an entire operations plant of 400 people, we held our first class for the night shift employees. Here's a list of things that went wrong:

1) Some of the students did not even know how to use a keyboard! Some had used Radio Frequency (RF) Scanners, but had never used a computer before. At the same time, within the first 10 minutes of a class, one of the students had already logged into the system using his iPhone! We did NOT know our audiences.

2) We had set up training laptops for the students, but due to poor communications, more people showed up to the class than laptops, so a few people had to double-up.

3) Prior to the class, we had created a training system, with dummy data, so that students could practice clicking through realistic scenarios during the class. However, we had not practiced the exact training scenarios in that training system; we had practiced using the real system. As a result, many of the class examples left the students with error messages. The training system didn't have enough data in it to run the reports in the scenarios. So, for many reports, students would receive the error message "insufficient data to run report."

4) During the class, some students (very politely) pointed out that our job aids did not exactly match what we were actually doing in the system. The problem, we realized, was that our job aids had been created weeks earlier, prior to the rollout of several system code changes. So, the screen and fields looked different.

5) We had not included process flowcharts as a part of the training. What we didn't count on was how the system required certain steps to be taken in a very specific order. However, on the manufacturing floor, the actual steps had been in a different order. That mistake led to a great deal of confused and stressful discussions during the class — and those conversations should have taken place weeks or months earlier!

6) At the end of the class, we handed out evaluation forms, but we did not lead a discussion with the students to help us improve the class. Due to that mistake, polite and timid students gave us average numerical ratings for the class, but we did not capture learnings to improve.

Our software system was excellent; our training was poor. Almost four months after the system had been rolled out, our Company's customers had stopped receiving their orders and shelves in supermarkets that should have been full with our salad dressings (and other products) were bare.

The customer complaints poured in. Even our Board of Directors convened a special meeting with our senior leadership team to ask why the Company's performance was so poor.

The software system worked fine. However, the

employees were so confused by the system that they stopped using it. Production Schedulers input orders into the system and line manufacturing employees just marked the orders complete; however, these manufacturing employees did not enter all the steps that the system had required. As an example, many of the Forklift Drivers would pick up and drop off boxes of products, without entering these orders into the system. So, we did not know where our products were, and we did not know how many cases were available nor how many cases had been shipped to customers.

I did not lose my job, fortunately. However, our entire project team received “unsatisfactory” performance ratings that year, and none of us received our bonuses.

I will listen to our Director of Training, every time, from now on!!

Story 5

We had such an amazing interview with Deborah, who told us this deliciously horrible presentation experience! Although it wasn't technically a training session (but rather a presentation), the story has several crucial lessons that apply to training — since most training does include carefully developed slides and other materials.

For this story, we do NOT learn the typical story of "always double-check your materials before the session," but rather we learn the painfully truthful story that even with the highest levels of attention to preparation, things go horribly wrong. There's no "Disney-ending" to this story; so, if you need a happy ending to your stories, perhaps move to the next chapter. But, if you want to vicariously experience a painful presentation, and perhaps glean some lessons or even sympatico-comfort, please enjoy…or, well, experience.

In our careers, we all will stumble and fall flat on our face at numerous points. Stay strong and majestic!

I am a Senior Vice President of Talent Management for a Fortune 500 company, with over 80,000 employees, and a CEO with a reputation for being tough and not too impressed with "HR People." I'm sure many of you can relate.

I have had many successful experiences at the Company, and continue to, as they say, "knock it out of the park" from time-to-time. But, when Jim asked me to tell him my most painful story of failure, a few options immediately came to mind — still, this one took the cake…

For over two years, I pushed and negotiated with our CEO to let us launch an Employee Engagement survey for our 80,000 employees. We had led a few surveys over the last 15 years, and prior to my joining the Company, but none were well-sponsored, and so they did not achieve business improvements. As such, the surveys stopped, and we haven't had a meaningful gauge of our employees for over six years. I was going to change that!

I lobbied for the money and sponsorship to ire a top notch firm to help us deliver our Employee ngagement survey. After gaining informal support from ll of the Company's senior business executives, I was eady to present to our CEO. And that presentation went ell! I received my budget, and he admitted that while e didn't see the value of the survey, he understood that was something that was needed. So, we got the green-ght, and I was thrilled.

For over eight months, we defined the survey,

communicated it, launched it, and finally we were ready to receive the results. As it turned out, our Senior Executive offsite was taking place in London just 3.5 weeks after the survey closed. Now, I know that telling you a number like 3.5 weeks is pretty specific. The reason I need to be that specific, is because it affects this story.

You see, our world-class consulting group had committed, through the RFP process ("Request For Proposal" process), to having all results within 1.5 MONTHS of the close of the survey. So, what I was pushing for was to have a high-level deck, ready for the Senior Executive meeting, in 3.5 WEEKS, with the remainder of the detailed results to come 3 weeks later. Everyone was on pins-and-needles because of my request. They saw the value of this presentation to the 60 most Senior Executives in the company, but they knew that the slightest mistake in the data processing could cause confusion, or even damage the consulting firm's reputation…and mine, for that matter. The stakes were high! Still, I pushed forward, because I believe that we all need to push for results, and ask for forgiveness if we can't deliver. At least we will give it our best!

(Hmmm…I'm going to have to reflect on that philosophy at some point, as I continue to progress in my career.)

Since we didn't want to blindside the CEO with this presentation, we scheduled a meeting, one week before the big offsite, to cover the high-level slides, and we populated the slides with "dummy data," since the final slides with the actual numbers wouldn't be ready until 3 days before the presentation. We explained to the CEO that this data was just made-up to show him the format for our presentation and asked that he allow us to show him the actual data, real-time, during the London presentation with everyone else. The CEO agreed.

Once we had that support, we also knew that all slide presentations had to be sent to the Project Manager in the Business Strategy department, at least one full week prior to the London meeting. To get around that requirement, I sent her the "dummy slides" that I had just showed the CEO, with the explanation that the real slides would come just 3 days before the presentation.

We clearly communicated to the Strategy Project Manager, in person, that these were dummy numbers, and the actual deck would come in later. This advance deck was solely so she could transfer the structure of the PowerPoint slides into the consistent PowerPoint format that she was using for all presentations. She clearly communicated that she understood. Well…

3 days before the presentation, as promised, I forwarded our slides to the project manager, who confirmed receipt. I knew that I was going to have a dry-run a couple days before the actual presentation, so would have a chance to see her work then. So far, we were all prepared.

2 days before the London presentation, I held my dry-run appointment, but they were still having some udio-visual problems, so I could only see the first two slides, both of which looked fine, and it looked like the formatting had been successfully transferred.

What I didn't know was that the project manager was not great with PowerPoint, and was having trouble copying the slides from one format to another.

Understandably, she did not let us know that, because she wanted everyone to think that she was on top of the offsite details.

So, what the project manager did was to manually copy all of the numbers and text from the dummy presentation into the final presentation. This involved literally dozens of "copy and paste" functions, and, as you can imagine, that left a great deal of room for errors. However, the final slides all LOOKED like they were correct — most of the "copy and paste" functions had been successful. What I didn't notice is that about 1/3 of those functions were unsuccessful. That meant that the survey results for the company were about 35% dead wrong!!

The London offsite had been moving along successfully for two days, and only of a few of the Company's select senior leaders were allowed the honor to present — and I was included in that short list. I was excited to say the least.

I had spent one hour each night, in my London hotel room, practicing my speech, and writing down all of the notes for the big talk. I was prepared for any question. I knew what to say, and I had even developed jokes specific to certain survey results.

I think you know where this is going already…

It was my turn. I walked up the front of the ballroom to explain the results for the first Employee Engagement survey the Company had ever implemented No one had seen these results, not even the CEO.

I began my talk and the first two slides went

flawlessly. The third slide had the "meat" of the presentation — this included our high-level "best and worst" survey questions, and the overall effectiveness of our company. As I walked the Senior Executives through the results, I had the sinking feeling that something was off — my notes were not matching these results. All of the sudden, I was not so confident in what to say, and I could hear my normally strong, confident voice quiver just a little bit.

The CEO began grilling me about these survey results. And, particularly, one element of the slide that was incorrect. In the dummy data, we had included as the Company's weakest question, a low response to the question "I have the intent to stay and work at this company for a long period of time." In actuality, the Company results on that question were excellent, and far above the Engagement Survey consulting firm's normative data. But, the Project Manager had not changed that piece of the dummy data, and it now showed up as 40% of the Company stated that they would only intend to stay at the company for less than one year — a tragic result, *if* that were accurate!

I stumbled and didn't know how to stop the presentation and say, "Sorry everyone, these slides are inaccurate. I should have checked them before walking in this morning. Let's take a 10min break and we'll update them." That would have been one, strong option for behaving. The other option was to "roll with it," and hope this presentation ended soon. I went with the latter.

The CEO was relentless. He continued to dig into that inaccurate question, and I finally explained that our results, compared to the consulting firm's normative data for that question, WERE quite good. That was true — and it answered the question partially. It was enough to move the CEO off the question. Fortunately, I was able to highlight the 65% of the survey results that were, indeed, accurate. I made it off the stage, but not without some damage to my reputation.

There is no "great ending" to this story. It was rough. The world continues to spin successfully on its axis. The "lessons learned" from this story? Of course, check your materials and don't trust them to anyone. And, perhaps, always keep a final draft on a thumb drive in your pocket. But, that's pretty extreme. You have to trust your colleagues at some point.

I think the real lesson here is that one's career doesn't always just move in one direction. Sometimes, we stumble, we fall, and we even fall hard. At whatever level we are in an organization, we are human beings. Whether you're a Marketing Manager who makes a spelling error on a billboard, or a Finance Director who transposes two numbers and causes incorrect data to be sent to IRS auditors, or a CEO who presents these faulty numbers to Wall Street, humans make errors.

I guess forgiveness of others and of ourselves is the key — particularly if we're giving it our ALL!

Your Notes: What did you learn from these stories? How will these failures help you to develop your future training projects?

Tips	
Cascading Sponsor Communications	Use "Cascading Sponsorship" to communicate training. That is, the first email should be from the most senior business supporter (such as a VP of Operations or a CFO), explaining why s/he believes the training to be important. Use cascading messages from less senior business people (such as department heads) to help communicate training logistics, such as registration, class locations, and timing.
Dry Run	Conduct at least one "Dry Run" for your training, once everything is ready. Be sure to invite critical people who will point out the details that don't work. Examples of what to watch for during a Dry Run include PowerPoint errors, scenarios that are clumsy during implementation, and technical challenges. The Dry Run also is a place to practice the instructor's speaking points and timing for each section. It is helpful to assign one person the role of "note-taker" during the Dry Run.

Speaker's Notes	◎Whether you are the trainer or you hire someone to conduct training, write out Speaker's Notes for each section. ◎Speaker's Notes can be in bullet-point fashion — they help the instructor to be "intentional" in everything they say and do. The trainer should keep his/her notes with them while delivering the Pilot, and perhaps a few more sessions. ◎Remember to include transition comments between sections. Transition phrases are helpful for students to connect each section to the last, and to the bigger picture of the training.
Pilot Training	◎Beyond Dry-Runs, conduct a Pilot for your training, using a smaller, select group of attendees. ◎Criteria for the Pilot attendees should include: quick on the uptake of new materials, verbally facile and can provide feedback without much prompting, subject matter experts (SMEs) who can provide insight on specific topics such as new process changes. ◎Budget time, at least once per day, to facilitate a feedback section. ◎Use flip charts to capture feedback, and, if possible, assign a note-taker during the Pilot.
Logistics Plan	◎Use a detailed checklist as a logistics plan, and assign the plan to one person for overall responsibility. ◎ Logistics Plans should be as detailed as possible (see Appendix), and should include categories such as: training materials development, room set-up, a/v set-up, food and beverages, and more…

* Contact us at www.taflat.com to get electronic or editable versions of these tables.

Handy Tool – To Help with Visualizing/ Designing the Training

Course Name:

Estimated Course Duration:

Audience:

- Who are the key audience groups that will attend the training?

Learning Objectives:

- Describe what the training is attempting to accomplish.
- Use the information from the Training Approach template* to complete this section

Section Name	Timing	Learning Objectives	Activities	Speaking Notes	Materials
XX	*XX minutes*	*Describe the key learning objective for this section*	*What activity will best achieve your learning objective for this section? e.g. presentation, scenario and group discussion, quiz, interactive large-group discussion, visual display of correct actions, etc.*	*What are the talking notes that will aid you in facilitating the training?*	*What materials do you need to conduct this activity?*
Note: Be sure to include sections for: -Introduction -Breaks (optional) -Feedback, Wrap-up					

Communication Plan:

- *Use the table below* to plan out your communication of the training.*
- *This includes the what, the how, the when, and the who.*

Audience	Vehicle	Sender	Communication Objective	Key Message/ Description	Timing	Status
Executive Sponsor	One-on-One	Joan	Gain active executive sponsorship for project	Deliver importance of project and need for active executive sponsorship	Dec. 14	
<Be sure to use Cascading Sponsorship – that is, line up individuals at various levels to help you communicate your project's importance>						

* Contact us at www.taflat.com to get electronic or editable versions of these tables.

Section Four: Sustaining Skills & Knowledge

TRAIN HARD — BUT IT'S BACK ON THE FIELD WHERE IT COUNTS!

"No institution can possibly survive if it needs geniuses or supermen to manage it. It must be organized in such a way as to be able to get along under a leadership composed of average human beings."
Peter Drucker

One of the many things that make Peter Drucker a great thinker is that he focuses more on systems and behavior, rather than on mood and personality. That is, organizations can and should be structured in such a way that strong leadership flourishes, even with regular people in leadership roles. And defining and supporting systems and behaviors are essential to sustaining the skills of a training program.

Whether your training focuses on soft skills or technical skills, that training is just a moment in time — it's back on the job where the skills are developed, and encouraged. If the skills are developed and supported, the learner will continue to practice and improve. Otherwise, the student will make honest commitments during the training session and then, again with the best intent, will forget all memory of these commitments within a few weeks, or months, or even days back on the job.

If you've ever broken a new year's resolution, you understand this point:

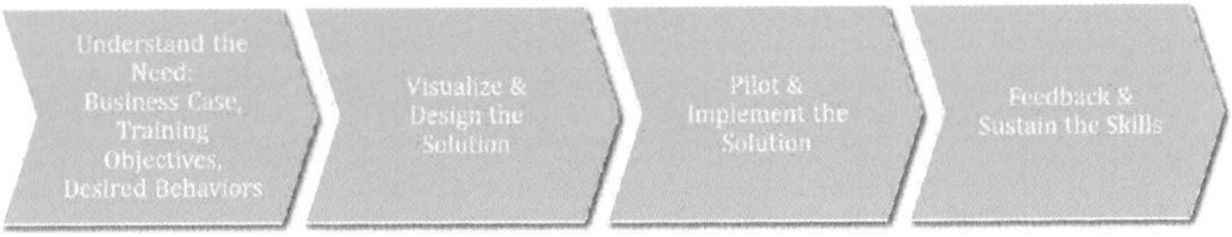

STRATEGIC PHASES OF TRAINING

If you recall, earlier in this book, we discussed that Phase One of your training program involves meeting with your business leader and facilitating a rich conversation with them about the business need behind the training.

In the "Tips" section for Phase One, we recommended defining **specific behaviors that the leader hopes to gain through the training**. We mentioned that this list would be critical in defining the curriculum and will be invaluable during the training to emphasize the purpose of the training for the students and the expectations. Even beyond this purpose, that list of specific behaviors can be used here to develop your Skill Sustainment Strategy.

For example, let's say your team is developing training around a significant change in the company's financial process, such as stricter compliance with the Sarbanes-Oxley Act, which regulates the financial processes and disclosures of public companies. All of the individuals in the finance department will need to understand exactly what is required of them to rollout and sustain the new process. In addition, the Sarbanes-Oxley process changes are likely to involve how the Sales department communicates their customers' orders to the Operations team. Across these departments, the employees must first agree on what great and effective communication looks like. Then, they will need to define specific service-level agreements, to define the time to complete activities across departments and between roles. In short, the specific communication behaviors, captured up front prior to developing the training, now become the communication scorecard for how well people are complying with the new process.

Carefully defining the new, necessary behaviors up-front will help you to develop both your curriculum and your post-training tracking and feedback.

Or, for another example, let's say the training that your team is delivering intends to support specific leadership behaviors, such as effective coaching of direct reports and delegation. In that case, you may consider altering your company's Performance Management process to reflect and measure those specific, new coaching behaviors. You may go even further and modify the entire Performance Management process, shifting to frequent manager-employee coaching meetings, which require the use of a specific coaching template -- the one taught in your classes.

Whatever your goals are for training, sustaining those specific behaviors is paramount, and, as Peter Drucker stated, the way to sustain behaviors is to set up the processes and structures that encourage those behaviors.

In our interviews with trainers, no other phase received as many stories of failure as this Sustainment Phase. In fact, this phase had nearly four times the number of stories of failure.

We selected this next story from a trainer who rolled out "Situational Leadership" training to the entire company's management staff. Situational Leadership is Ken Blanchard's framework for breaking down jobs into tasks, and adjusting your coaching style for each individual task. Once leaders learn this technique, they should be able to adjust their coaching styles depending on each of their individual direct report's needs. For example, a leader will provide more directive, detailed instructions on tasks that are new for an employee and will allow for more freedom on tasks on which the employee has displayed mastery. It's a great model.

This trainer explained to us that while her training was considered excellent at the time of the training, one year after the training…well, you can hear the story from her.

Story 6

I did everything right…well, almost everything. In planning to deliver Situational Leadership training (Ken Blanchard's leadership techniques) to 800 of our Company's leaders who managed direct reports, I set up a Steering Committee to help me define the behaviors we hoped to see. Then, my team and I hired a few more training consultants, planned our training, and within four months, we were ready to launch the training program. And, it went great!

Our external training consultants delivered fun and dynamic training, and the leaders said that they liked he new leadership model and simple techniques. I was hrilled. We charged forward and, for the next year, we lelivered this two-day course to all 800 leaders. What ould go wrong?!

Well, what I had not counted on was just how nuch people tend to forget after training! And we had not efined any Skill Sustainment Plan.

So, one year after all-implementation-all-the-time, had a moment to pause and wonder just how much our ourse participants were learning from the training. Since our Steering Committee of Senior Executives had been so engaged, I emailed them excitedly to let them know that I would be conducting a series of focus groups, and then would schedule a Steering Committee meeting with them to debrief and review the focus group results. I fully anticipated terrific results, so I didn't even plan much time between the focus groups' ending and the debrief meeting. Little did I know how appalled I was about to be!

To start, I conducted 4 focus groups. In each group, we started with an activity of breaking into small groups and, by memory, attempting to recreate the Situational Leadership model that we had spent a full 2-days learning during last year's training. Of the 12 small groups, only one group could successfully write out the elements of the model. Furthermore, of the 23 people who attended the focus groups, 21 people admitted outright that they had never actually used the model post-training.

As a success metric, I could only point to 2 leaders who were using the Situational Leadership model back on the job with their direct reports. Now, these two leaders had excitedly explained how helpful the model had been to their management style, and that their direct reports felt they were being effectively coached and mentored. As for the other 21 people in our focus groups, they couldn't recall more than a few concepts in the Situational Leadership model.

Now I had the task of reporting these results to the Steering Committee.

Well, I have learned in my career that when you have bad news to explain to senior executives, the best way is to present it fast and with full honesty. I prepared the slides with an executive summary slide at the start, stating that while our training was immediately perceived by the participants as valuable, our post-training analysis points to a lack of "stickiness" of the training. That is, the specific leadership coaching skills and techniques did not stay with the participants after the training sessions ended. You can imagine how painful this discussion was to prepare for.

Your Notes: What did you learn from this story? How will this failure help you to develop your future training projects?

I'd like to leave you with one thought from this book:

Cherish and share your failures.

These experiences will shape the success of your career.

And, if you're in the middle of a disaster, pause, smile, and ask yourself,

"What am I meant to learn from this stress?"

On a longer timeline, our "stress" may be the experience that launches your executive career.

Tips	
Start with the end in mind: ***Know the business sponsor's training objectives – for example, specific behaviors and how they will increase the value of the business***	◯ Work with your business sponsor to establish the business objective. ◯ Get down to the behavioral level – to understand what are the behaviors this business sponsor wants to witness when his/her staff gets back on the job (i.e. post-training).
Use those business objectives and behaviors to plan your sustainment activities	◯ The hardest part of training is convincing the business sponsor and the training participants that they need to work after the training to fold the skills into their work. ◯ By using the business sponsor's own thoughts, you will find it easier to persuade them to put more effort into capturing training skills and reinforcing those skills in the organization.
Culture Fit	◯ Make sure your sustainment activity fits with the culture – try to add it to something that is already accepted and done. ◯ As trainers, we all want our training to be the #1 most important thing for the organization. We need to check ourselves, because if we push a little bit too much, we could lose it all. Push, but remain flexible and listen carefully to the "rumblings" out there.

Handy Tool – To Help with Sustaining Skills and Knowledge

Use the table below* to decide on which Sustainment lan works best for your initiative:

Sustainment Plan	Description	Pros	Cons	Key Success Factors
Individual Project	Requires that the learner develop a project, either during or immediately after the training, that represents how they will use the training content.	Tremendous way to transfer accountability for learning. Provides the opportunity for learners to contemplate the curriculum and their jobs.	Whenever a student is asked to do something, there has to be a way to hold them accountable. Requires Sponsorship. Requires communication.	Whatever the learner decides to use, the learner is required to share the plan with their manager within a week of the training's ending.
Performance Management	Build the training skills into the next Performance Evaluation.	Holds leaders accountable to use what they learned. Displays the business value of the training.	Goals can be hard to write and hard to measure. Adds more goals to "the list" evaluations.	Make sure that the individual knows that the skill will be added to their next Performance Evaluation.
Leadership Behaviors	Creates 4-5 Leadership Behaviors for all leaders in the company.	May have a set of core Leadership Behaviors as well as customized behaviors for specific management levels.	Behaviors that are not carefully defined, with examples of success, can create confusion in an organization. Requires communication.	Define who is a "leader" in the company (i.e. are they "Managers and Above" or "Anyone who manages people"?). Define these leadership behaviors with senior staff involvement

* Contact us at www.taflat.com to get electronic or editable versions of these tables.

FURTHER RESOURCES

The Impact of Learning through Failure

Although many executives believe that all failure is bad and that learning from failure experiences is relatively straightforward, failures in organizational life are inevitable and can even be good. Successful learning from failure, however, is not a simple process — it requires context-specific strategies that start with understanding the disadvantages to the "blame game" and working to create an organizational culture that permits employees to report and admit failure.

Failure experiences fall into three categories: 1) preventable failures in predictable operations, 2) unavoidable failures in complex systems, and 3) intelligent failures at the frontier. This last kind of failure is the ideal — they are small and occur quickly, providing the most valuable information and offer opportunities to experiment proactively.

Edmonson, A. C. (2011, April). Strategies for learning from failure. *Harvard Business Review.*

◆

Most of us remember negative events more strongly and in more detail than we do positive events. This happens for both physiological and psychological reasons. The negative emotions that are associated with negative events generally involve more thinking — the information is processed more thoroughly than for positive emotions. Further, we tend to use stronger words to describe unpleasant events and emotions and we tend to ruminate more about them. Moreover, we tend to consider people who say negative things as smarter than those who say positive things, and we are more likely to give weight to critical reviews of our work and ourselves. In other words, these negative events and emotions wear off more slowly than the good ones do.

There is an evolutionary basis for why this happens. In our evolutionary history, those who were more attuned to the bad signs and events in life were more likely to survive the numerous threats to survival and would have therefore been more likely to pass along their genes.

Tugend, A. (2012, March). Praise is fleeting, but brickbats we recall. *The New York Times*.

◆

Learning from Others' Mistakes

"Intelligence is the ability to learn from your mistakes. Wisdom is the ability to learn from the mistakes of others." – Anonymous

◆

According to recent findings from researchers at the University of Bristol in England, what sticks with us is not our peers' successes, but rather their failures. Volunteers of the study played a simple game against a computer-controlled competitor. Players had to choose one of four boxes, each of which had varying sums of money inside — in order to maximize their winnings, players had to occasionally sample every one of the boxes.

Interestingly, when players saw their computer-competitor win an unexpectedly high sum, their fMRI scans showed no reactionary measurable brain activity. However, when the computer-competitor received a surprisingly low sum, the parts of our brains associated with inhibition lit up in the players.

Paul Howard-Jones, who co-led the study with fellow researcher Rafal Bogaez, sums up the lesson from this study — learning from competition "is not learning to act like your competitor, it is learning not to act like your competitor when they fail."

Swaminathan, N. (2011, January). Monkey see, monkey don't: Learning from others' mistakes. *Scientific American*.

◆

Embracing Failure

Although failure may be inevitable, it can actually be very useful…but only if managed well. The right amount of failure cannot only let you find out what *doesn't* work, but it can also help you keep your options open, attract resources and attention, allow room for new leaders, and develop intuition and skill.

What is the right amount of failure then? It involves failing intelligently. It involves failing fast and failing cheaply. For example, you can decide what success and failure look like respectively before you start a project. And lastly, it involves failing and then sharing what you learned with others.

McGrath, R. G. (2011, April). Failing by design. *Harvard Business Review.*

◆

Experiencing Failure Leads to Success

"I've missed more than 9,000 shots in my career. I've lost almost 300 games. 26 times, I've been trusted to take the game winning shot and missed. I've failed over and over and over again in my life. And that is why I succeed." — Michael Jordan

◆

Every experience is a learning opportunity, but xperiencing failure teaches us in a unique way that uccess does not

Part of this is because of the strong emotional omponent involved with failing. Much like how smell vokes the most powerful memories, strong negative eelings like shame, regret, and embarrassment are ncompassed within our memories of our biggest nistakes and therefore teach us powerful lessons.

Experiencing failure teaches us not only about the specific process and product of that one experience, but also more general skills that we can carry throughout our daily lives. These skills include: 1) how to reflect, 2) how to fix mistakes, 3) how to stop being defensive, 4) how to set intention, and 5) how to be resilient.

Ryan, L. (2015, December). Five lessons only failure can teach you. *Forbes*.

◆

Although it is common to feel frustration after experiencing failure, such experiences are also a powerful catalyst to developing new knowledge and enhancing innovation within organizations. In order to reap these benefits of failure, organizations need to have the capacity to learn from their failures. With enough capacity, people can learn from failure in two important ways. Firstly, people can learn from direct experiences of failure, which increases innovation agility. Secondly, people can learn from vicarious experiences of failure, which enhances product innovation outcomes, such as patents.

Carmeli, A. & Dothan, A. (2017). Generative Work Relationships as a Source of Direct and Indirect Learning From Experiences of Failure: Implications for Innovation Agility and Product Innovation. Technological Forecasting and Social Change: *An International Journal*, 119.

◆

Learning through Stories of Failure versus Stories of Success

Researchers Bledow, Carette, Kühnel, and Bister argue that other people's failures offer a generally neglected resource for managerial learning. Stories of failures are differentiated from those of success by their negative emotional impact. This negativity elicits more pronounced motivational responses in learners so that they elaborate the content of failure stories more actively than they do for success stories. Because of this, learning from failure stories results in more elaboration and learning transfer, which has powerful implications for managerial and personal learning in educational and organizational settings.

Bledow, R., Bernd, C., Kühnel, J., & Bister, D. (2017). Learning from Others' Failures: The Effectiveness of Failure Stories for Managerial Learning. *The Academy of Management Learning & Education*, 16(1), 39-53.

◆

Many people enjoy the experience of being afraid – anyone who enjoys watching horror films or riding ollercoasters can tell you about this thrill. The natural igh of our fight-or-flight response can feel great in a lood of adrenaline, endorphins, and dopamine. In fact, ese chemicals released during flight-or-flight can work ke glue to build the strong memories referred to as lashbulb memories."

Interestingly, humans have been scaring emselves and each other throughout the evolution of our species. We have used many different methods (storytelling, cliff jumping, sky diving, etc.) and for many different reasons. Three of these reasons are 1) to prepare our children for like in the real world, 2) to control behavior, and 3) to build group unity. In fact, we build a special closeness with those who are with us when we are in an excited, frightened state. We need each other in times of stress and our bodies have subsequently evolved to ensure that we feel that closeness with our companions when that stress occurs. Therefore, the powerful thrill that we feel during these moments of stress and fear work to make memories stick in our brains and to make us stick together.

Ringo A. (2013, October). Why do some brains enjoy fear? The science behind the appeal of haunted houses, freak shows, and physical thrills. *The Atlantic*.

◆

Four major things occur to our brains while listening to someone telling a story. Firstly, the story activated parts of the brain that envisions the story in the listener's own ideas and experiences. This is called "neural coupling." Secondly, this neural coupling prompts dopamine to be released into the system as it experiences the emotionally charged events of the story. This increase in dopamine makes it easier for us to remember stories and concepts with greater accuracy.

Thirdly, in what is referred to as "mirroring," listeners not only experience similar brain activity to the storyteller, but also share the exact same brain activity. I other words, when one person tells a story to an active listener, their brains actually begin to synchronize. When this mirroring occurs, it is possible for the listener to even anticipate the speaker's brain activity! And fourthly, two areas of the brain are activated while it processes the facts. While listening to a story, the brain is engaged in many additional areas, including the motor cortex, the sensory cortex, and the frontal cortex. This increased activation is what captures and engages us while also more thoroughly ingraining the story in our memories.

Dooley, R. (2010). *Stories Synchronize Brains*. Neuromarketing by Roger Dooley (et al).

24135335R00049

Printed in Great Britain
by Amazon